Toni Morrison's

THE BLUEST EYE

Adapted

by

LYDIA R. DIAMOND

Dramatic Publishing

Woodstock, Illinois • England • Australia • New Zealand

IMPORTANT BILLING AND CREDIT REQUIREMENTS

All producers of the play *must* give credit to Toni Morrison as the author of the book and Lydia Diamond as the dramatizer of the play in all programs distributed in connection with performances of the play and in all instances in which the title of the play appears for purposes of advertising, publicizing or otherwise exploiting the play and/or a production. The names of Toni Morrison and Lydia Diamond *must* also appear on a separate line, on which no other name appears, immediately following the title, and *must* appear in size of type not less than fifty percent (50%) the size of the title type. Biographical information on Toni Morrison and Lydia Diamond, if included in the playbook, may be used in all programs. *In all programs this notice must appear:*

In addition, all producers of the play must include the following announcement on the title page of all programs distributed in connection with performances of the play and on all advertising and promotional materials:

"*The Bluest Eye* was commissioned and developed through the
Steppenwolf for Young Adults and the New Plays Initiative
by Steppenwolf Theatre Company, Chicago, Illinois
(Martha Lavey, Artistic Director,
David Hawkanson, Executive Director),
where it received its world premiere in February 2005."

PLAYWRIGHT'S NOTE

I am so pleased to have played a part in bringing Toni Morrison's exquisitely rendered novel to audiences in a new way and will always be appreciative that she agreed to let it have this new life. The process of adapting this piece has been challenging and rewarding. The journey has been a playwright's dream, an initial production in a safe and nurturing environment with brilliant theater artists followed by more readings and productions with generous, talented and smart collaborators. I cannot begin to thank everyone who has helped shape this piece, so I will limit myself to the people who touched it first: the Steppenwolf Theatre Company; Lenora Inez Brown, the play's first dramaturge; Hallie Gordon, the amazing director of its two productions at Steppenwolf and then at The New Vic in New York; David Muse, with whom I got to workshop the piece in between Steppenwolf productions and who eventually directed a thoughtful and elegant production at Theatre Alliance in Washington, D.C., and finally, two other illuminating productions—Playmakers Rep in North Carolina and Plowshares Theatre Company in Detroit.

I'd like to share a couple of lessons I've learned along the way. Actors and directors can easily get pulled into a maddening process of trying to separate the "kid" voices from the "mature narration" handled by Claudia and Frieda. It's an understandable dilemma, as so many narrative passages are said with a hindsight and sophistication not readily evident in the playful dialogue exchanges. Not only are Frieda and Claudia precocious, but also there is a convention that allows the characters subtle shifts in maturity and tone independent of vocal variances. The play works best when the young narrators retain a mature, natural, conversational tone and rhythm when addressing the audience and each other. (Also, we have a tendency to underestimate the rich emotional and verbal life of young adults…the play is quite purposeful in its attempt to honor the sophisticated, syncopated rhythms of young speech.)

I worked hard in this adaptation to approach the story as a tale of the damaging trickle-down effect of a rather crippling societal racism, not merely as the story of a dysfunctional family and community. I feel strongly that this most serves the intention of the book and also serves the dramatic intention of the play. To this end, I think it is very important that the piece be spared graphic, realistic representations of sexual violence. As soon as we are made to watch a heinous act of incest on stage, we are forced to assimilate that act first and foremost. We lose sight of its place in the story and ultimately end up diminishing the tragic effect of the act itself as well as obscuring Pecola's story.

Thank you for your interest in this work.

Toni Morrison's *The Bluest Eye* was commissioned by Steppenwolf Theatre Company, Chicago, Ill. (Martha Lavey, Artistic Director and David Hawkanson, Executive Director), where it received its world premiere in February 2005.

The production was directed by Hallie Gordon, the assistant director was Jocelyn Prince, with scenic design by Stephanie Nelson, costume design by Alison Heryer, lighting design by J.R. Lederle, sound design by Victoria Delorio, dramaturgy by Lenora Inez Brown, choreography by Ann Boyd and casting by Erica Daniels. The stage manager was Deb Styer.

CAST

Claudia:	Libya V. Pugh
Frieda & Darlene:	Monifa M. Days
Pecola Breedlove:	Alana Arenas
Mama:	TaRon Patton
Pauline Breedlove:	Chavez Ravine
Soaphead Church:	Sati Word
Cholly Breedlove:	Phillip Edward Van Lear
Maureen Peal:	Noelle Hardy

Steppenwolf Theatre Company remounted the production in Chicago in October 2006; the New York City premiere of Steppenwolf's production was subsequently presented in November 2006 by The New 42nd Street at The Duke on 42nd Street. In the remount, James Vincent Meredith (Soaphead Church & Daddy) and Victor J. Cole (Cholly Breedlove) joined the cast. Beth Stegman was the assistant stage manager.

THE BLUEST EYE

A Play in Three Acts

CHARACTERS

CLAUDIA: Precocious, sensitive girl. She must be able to move gracefully between the innocence of youth and the wisdom of the narrator who has lived through it all. Dexterity with direct address a must.

FRIEDA/DARLENE: Claudia's older sister. Somewhat more practical than Claudia. Possibly more stern, slightly less personable.

PECOLA: A shy, quiet, resigned and somewhat pained presence. She should be completely innocent. We must love her and want to take care of her, but not pity her. Perhaps there is a certain quiet pride that won't let us tip over into pity. It is imperative that she have very dark brown skin.

MAMA: She possesses an imposing presence. She loves her children and this should be evident despite her stern manner.

MRS. BREEDLOVE: An older version of Pecola, also dark brown. Painfully shy and insecure, and still very adept at addressing the audience.

DADDY/SOAPHEAD CHURCH: Charismatic, odd, charming, mature.

CHOLLY: Mrs. Breedlove's age, the shell of a man who may have been physically impressive at one time, dark brown complexion.

MAUREEN PEAL/WHITE GIRL: Light skinned, very pretty. More complicated than merely "snotty." She is a real person, as complicated as the other characters.

Note; The children are played by adults. Women 1, 2 and 3 can be played by any of the women available.

ACT I

Scene i

(Lights rise on PECOLA standing, dwarfed in a splash of light. She wears a dingy loose fitting white dress with a matching bow in her hair, she holds a large red book. She opens it and reads to audience:)

PECOLA. Here is the house. It is green and white. It has a red door. It is very pretty.

(MRS. BREEDLOVE and CHOLLY enter.)

MRS. BREEDLOVE & CHOLLY. Here is the family, Mother, Father, Dick and Jane live in the green-and-white house.

(FRIEDA and CLAUDIA enter. As cast members enter their voices join the chant at a point it is frenetic, no longer in unison.)

FRIEDA & CLAUDIA. They are very happy. *(Add MAUREEN.)* See Jane. She has a red dress. She wants to play. Who will play with Jane? *(MAMA.)* See Mother. Mother is very nice. Mother, will you play with Jane? *(Add CHOLLY.)* See Father. He is big and strong. Father will you play with Jane? Father is smiling. Smile, Father, smile. *(Add SOAPHEAD.)* See the dog. Bow-wow goes the dog. Do you want to play with Jane?

PECOLA. Look, look. Here comes a friend. The friend will play with Jane. They will play a good game.

(PECOLA turns, we see in profile that she is pregnant, she closes the primer. Lights and sound out.)

Scene ii

(Lights rise. CLAUDIA stands DR, holding FRIEDA's hand. She wears an orange dress much like PECOLA's dingy white. A matching bow in her hair. FRIEDA's dress is brown. Autumn.)

CLAUDIA. Quiet as it's kept, there were no marigolds in the fall of 1941. Not even the gardens fronting the lake showed marigolds that year. We thought, at the time, it was because Pecola was having her father's baby that the marigolds did not grow. We had dropped our seeds in our own little plot of black dirt, just as Pecola's father had dropped his seeds in his own plot of black dirt.

FRIEDA. The seeds shriveled and died; Pecola's baby too. *(Beat.)* There is really nothing more to say—except why.

CLAUDIA. But since why is difficult to handle, one must take refuge in how.

(Lighting changes.)

FRIEDA. Pecola came to us in autumn.

(PECOLA appears, her dingy dress now cinched at the waist by the bow that was in her hair. She carries a large, worn paper bag, and stands in the same spot. She is the embodiment of loneliness and dejection...one dingy sock is up, the other around her ankle...her shoulders are slumped and her head down.)

CLAUDIA. In autumn school starts and Frieda and I get new brown stockings and cod-liver oil. Daddy spends hours cutting and stacking.

DADDY. You need to make sure the wood is stacked perpendicular...

FRIEDA. Perpin...?

CLAUDIA. That's up and down, not sideways...

FRIEDA. I knew that. *(To audience.)* I did.

DADDY. What you need to do is make sure the pieces on top slant down so the rain slides off. Not gonna stay warm on damp wood.

CLAUDIA. Daddy goes on and on...

DADDY. And damp wood makes moldy wood,

CLAUDIA. And on...

DADDY. and moldy wood's no good, presents a whole n'other set of problems. Remember kindling goes in the bucket under

CLAUDIA & FRIEDA. And on...

DADDY. the shed. Kindling has to stay dry. And, girls, remember if it's not smaller than your ring finger,

FRIEDA, CLAUDIA & DADDY. it's not kindling.

DADDY *(overlapping MAMA)*. What you need to do is make sure the flue's clean before the first frost...if you wait you got yourself a mess, and...

MAMA. Lord, if it's not one thing it's the other. It's cold. Girls. Girls? Are you listening to me?

DADDY. Are you listening to me?

CLAUDIA. Mama has Frieda stuff rags in the window to stave off the cold.

FRIEDA. And we collect the coal that falls off of the trains onto the railroad tracks.

DADDY. You need to get the medium-sized pieces... Small pieces turn to dust, won't help us none, you need the medium pieces that fall from the top of the heap. Make sure you keep your eyes up and your ears open, no piece of coal's worth a flattened girl.

FRIEDA. Staving off the cold is a family project.

CLAUDIA. And I get a cold anyway. *(Sneezes.)*

MAMA. Great Jesus.

FRIEDA. That's what she always does in the fall.

CLAUDIA. I get sick and Mama fusses.

(Light fades on PECOLA. Light in different area rises on MAMA, she fusses, partially under CLAUDIA's words.)

MAMA. Get on in that bed. How many times do I have to tell you to wear something on your head? You must be the biggest fool in this town. Frieda?

FRIEDA. Yes ma'am?

MAMA. Stuff that window and get the cod-liver oil. Lord, If I ain't told Claudia once I ain't told her a thousand times, keep that jacket on when the weather starts to cool. Frieda,

FRIEDA. Yes ma'am?

MAMA. Get me the Vicks salve. *(MAMA's words continue under CLAUDIA's.)* I know I don't work my fingers to the bone so my childrens can be laid up in bed sick. Next thing I know, Claudia done pass it to Frieda then we all sick. Lord have mercy and help us all.

CLAUDIA. I lie in the bed. No one speaks to me or asks how I feel. When I throw up Mama says...

MAMA. What did you puke on the bedclothes for? Frieda...

FRIEDA. Yes, Mama?

MAMA. Get me the clean sheet from the line. Don't you have sense enough to hold your head out of the bed? Now, look what you did. You think I got time for nothing but washing up your puke? *(MAMA continues to fuss, soundlessly.)*

CLAUDIA. Mama's voice drones on. She is not talking to me. She is talking to the puke, but she is calling it my name.

MAMA. Claudia, Claudia, Claudia, Lord knows I don't have time for wiping up after girls without enough since to puke outta the side of the bed...

CLAUDIA. But maybe it wasn't that bad.

(MAMA's gestures soften.)

MAMA. Frieda, I said get me the Vick's salve.

FRIEDA. Yes ma'am.

MAMA. And some flannel.

FRIEDA. Yes ma'am.

CLAUDIA. Mama's hands are large and rough. She takes two fingers full of the salve at a time and massages it into my chest until I am faint. Just when I think I will tip over into a scream she scoops out a little and puts it in my mouth, telling me to—

MAMA. Swallow.

CLAUDIA. She wraps the flannel around my neck and chest and covers me up with heavy quilts.

MAMA. Now sweat, Claudia.

CLAUDIA. —which I do promptly.

FRIEDA. But it wasn't all bad.

CLAUDIA. Mama meant well. In our household there was love. Love from Mama and Daddy, thick and dark as Alaga syrup. I could smell it—taste it—sweet, musty, with an edge of wintergreen in its base. It stuck, along with my tongue, to the frosted windowpanes. When the flannel came undone in my sleep and I coughed dry and tough in the night, Daddy stood in the doorway while Mama's hands re-pinned the flannel and rested a moment on my forehead.

(MAMA's light fades.)

CLAUDIA. So when I think of autumn, I think of somebody with hands who does not want me to die.

FRIEDA. And Daddy's strong silhouette looking over us, quiet and serious and concerned.

CLAUDIA. And Pecola.

FRIEDA. That's right. Pecola Breedlove.

(PECOLA's light rises again. She looks up, a doe caught in the headlights.)

CLAUDIA. Yes. That's what I was trying to say, isn't it. That there was enough love in that house to give a little to Pecola, who was sorely in need of someone to care.

Scene iii

(PECOLA enters, pulls a primer out of her paper bag, opens it to a marked passage and begins to read:)

PECOLA. Here is the family. Mother, Father, Dick and Jane. They are very happy.

CLAUDIA. Mrs. Breedlove was a peculiar sort.

PECOLA. Come and play. Come play with Jane.

(Light rises on MRS. BREEDLOVE standing in same spot Claudia and Frieda's mother stood in earlier. She wears a pristine maid's uniform.)

FRIEDA. All of the Breedloves were peculiar.

CLAUDIA. Frieda!

FRIEDA. It's true. Peculiar and funny looking.

MRS. BREEDLOVE. When I had my girl, I 'member I said I'd love it no matter what it looked like.

(PECOLA kneels, clasps her hands in prayer.)

CLAUDIA. Actually the Breedloves were not ugly so much as they were just poor and black and believed that they were ugly.

FRIEDA. They were peculiar.

CLAUDIA. You already said that.

FRIEDA. Well, they were.

PECOLA. Please, God. Please make me disappear. Please, please, please, please, God.

FRIEDA. Peculiar like they lived in a storefront 'stead of a regular house.

CLAUDIA. And Pecola called her mother Mrs. Breedlove.
FREIDA & CLAUDIA. Peculiar.
MRS. BREEDLOVE. I went to the hospital when my time
    come. Didn't want to have it at home. They put me in a
    big room with a whole mess of women. The pains was
    coming, but not too bad. The doctors come to examine
    me.
PECOLA. Please, God. Make me invisible... Please,
    please, please, please, please, please...

*(PECOLA's pleads of "please" are whispered under
MRS. BREEDLOVE's...)*

MRS. BREEDLOVE. One old doctor was learning the
    young ones about babies. When he got to me he said,
    now these here women you don't have any trouble with.
    They deliver right away with no pain. Just like horses.
CLAUDIA. Pecola's pain antagonized me. I wanted to
    open her up, crisp her edges, ram a stick down that
    hunched and curving spine. I wanted to force her to
    stand erect and spit the misery out on the streets.
FRIEDA. But she held her misery where it could lap into
    her eyes.
PECOLA. Amen. *(Stands, to audience:)* If I squeeze my
    eyes shut, real tight, little parts of my body go away. I
    have to do it real slow like, then in a rush. First, off my
    fingers go, one by one, then my arms disappear, all the
    way to my elbows. My feet now. Yes that's right good.
    My legs go all at once. Above my thighs is the hardest
    part. I have to be real still and pull and pull and pull...
    when my stomach goes away the chest and neck follow

'long pretty easy. The face is hard too. Almost done, almost. But my eyes is always left.

MRS. BREEDLOVE. Only one of the doctor students ever looked at me, looked in my eyes. I looked right back at him. He dropped his eyes and turned red. He knowed, I reckon, that maybe I weren't no horse foaling.

PECOLA. It don't matter how hard I try, my eyes is always left. And I try. Every night I pray for God to deliver me blue eyes. I have prayed now going on a year, but I have hope still. I figure God is very busy, and I am very small. To have something wonderful as that happen would have to take a long, long time. Blue eyes like Shirley Temple, or Mary Jane, on the Mary Jane candies. Or Jane in the primer at school.

MRS. BREEDLOVE. I seed them doctors talking to them white women: "How you feel? Gonna have twins?" Nice friendly talk. When them pains got harder I moaned something awful. They wasn't as bad as I let on, but I had to let them people know having a baby was more than a bowel movement. I hurt just like them white women. Just 'cause I wasn't hooping and hollering didn't mean I wasn't feeling pain. They think just 'cause I knowed how to have a baby with no fuss that my behind wasn't pulling and aching like theirs? Besides, that doctor don't know what he talking about. He must never seed no mare foal. Who say they can't have no pain? Just 'cause she don't cry? 'Cause she cain't say it, they think it ain't there? If they look in her eyes and see them eyeballs lolling back, see the sorrowful look, they'd know. *(Beat.)* Anyways the baby come.

PECOLA. And people would have to be nice and the teachers would see me, they would really look at me in my eyes and say, look at pretty-eyed Pecola. We musn't do bad things in front of those pretty eyes. Pretty eyes. Pretty blue eyes. Big blue pretty eyes. I would be very happy, like Jane, and Shirley and the candy girl.

MRS. BREEDLOVE. She was a big ole healthy baby. All big brown eyes and hair. A right smart baby she was. I used to like to watch her nurse. You know they makes them greedy sounds when they nurse. Eyes all soft and wet, like a cross between a puppy and a dying man. But I knowed she was ugly, head full of pretty hair, but Lord she was ugly.

PECOLA. They are very happy.

(PECOLA closes the book. Lights fade.)

Scene iv

(CLAUDIA and FRIEDA cross to downstage. The BREEDLOVES stand near them.)

CLAUDIA. The Breedlove's ugliness was a unique kind of ugliness.

FRIEDA. No one could have convinced them that they were not relentlessly and aggressively ugly.

CLAUDIA. Except for Cholly,

FRIEDA. whose ugliness had more to do with his behavior…

CLAUDIA. Mrs. Breedlove and Pecola wore their ugliness, put it on, so to speak, although it did not belong to them.

FRIEDA. You looked at them and wondered why they were so ugly; you looked closely and could not find the source.

CLAUDIA. Then you realized it came from conviction. Their conviction. It was as though some mysterious all-knowing master had given each one a cloak of ugliness to wear, and they had each accepted it without question. The master had said, "You are ugly people." It was a truth supported by every billboard, every movie, every glance.

BREEDLOVES. "Yes,"

CLAUDIA. they had said.

BREEDLOVES. "You are right."

FRIEDA. And they took the ugliness in their hands, threw it as a mantle over them, *(BREEDLOVES put on sweaters/jackets, blankets)* and went about the world with it.

(The BREEDLOVES take their places. MRS. B. in the bed with CHOLLY, PECOLA in the other bed.)

CLAUDIA. On a Saturday morning in October, not much different from any other Saturday morning in October, they began, one by one, to stir out of their dreams of affluence and vengeance into the anonymous misery of their ugly storefront and ugly lives.

(MRS. BREEDLOVE gets out of bed and walks to the table. She makes a show of slamming plates onto the table.

CHOLLY mumbles, thrashes about in the bed for a moment and rolls over. MRS. BREEDLOVE makes even more noise. PECOLA sits up in bed. When the noise fails to wake up CHOLLY, MRS. BREEDLOVE goes to the bed.)

MRS. BREEDLOVE. I need some more coal. *(CHOLLY does not respond.)* I said, I need some more coal.

CHOLLY. Awwwww, woman!

MRS. BREEDLOVE. I need some coal now. It's cold! You so drunk you wouldn't feel hellfire, but I'm cold. I got to do a lot of things, but I ain't got to freeze.

CHOLLY. Leave me alone.

MRS. BREEDLOVE. If working like a mule don't give me the right to be warm, what am I doing it for? You sure don't bring in nothing. If it was up to you, we'd all be dead. If you think I'm gone wade out into the cold and get it myself, you'd better think again.

CHOLLY. I don't much care how you get it.

MRS. BREEDLOVE. You going to get your drunk self out of that bed and get me some coal or not? *(Silence.)* Cholly! *(Silence.)* Don't try me this morning, man. *(Silence.)* All right. All right. But if I sneeze once, just once, God help you!

FRIEDA. They all knew that Mrs. Breedlove could have, would have, and had, gotten coal from the shed. She might even have had Pecola do it.

CLAUDIA. This was a ceremonial dance. The orchestra was warming up. They waited in anticipation for the conductor's baton.

(Long moment of silence. MRS. BREEDLOVE sits at the table and waits. In slow motion she sneezes. The sneeze

is amplified and distorted. The effect is ominous and possibly amusing.

A highly choreographed slow-motion fight ensues under CLAUDIA's monologue. PECOLA rocks and covers herself with the blankets. The speed of the "dance" slows in opposition to the animation of CLAUDIA's words. The dance repeats itself. On her bed, PECOLA repeats the same physical process she showed us earlier for "making herself invisible."

The final image is that of CHOLLY knocked unconscious, MRS. BREEDLOVE standing over him.)

CLAUDIA. Cholly and Mrs. Breedlove fought each other with a darkly brutal formalism that was paralleled only by their lovemaking. Tacitly they had agreed not to kill each other. He fought her the way a coward fights a man—with feet, the palms of his hands, and teeth. She, in turn, fought back in a purely feminine way—with frying pans and pokers, and occasionally a flatiron would sail toward his head. They did not talk, groan, or curse during these beatings. There was only the muted sound of falling things, and flesh on unsurprised flesh.

(The fight, perhaps choreographed to a skewed instrumental of "Precious Lord," ends several beats after CLAUDIA's last word.

The music stops. Lighting reverts back to top of scene.)

MRS. BREEDLOVE. Pecola, now you go get me that coal.

Scene v

(PECOLA enters with brown paper bag. FRIEDA and CLAUDIA are playing hopscotch when she arrives.)

PECOLA. Whatchu doin'?

CLAUDIA. Playin'. Want to?

PECOLA. I'll watch.

FRIEDA. You might as well play. Claudia's no good competition anyhow.

CLAUDIA. Mama told us you here 'cause your Mama and Daddy went at it and then your Daddy burned up your house and now you outdoors.

FRIEDA. Claudia!

CLAUDIA. What? It's true. *(To PECOLA.)* It's true, isn't it?

PECOLA. I ain't outdoors, we just stayin' away for a minute while Mrs. Breedlove do some things 'round the house.

(Light changes.)

CLAUDIA *(to audience)*. I knew this was a falsehood. Frieda had heard people talkin'…

(WOMEN 1, 2 and 3 [played by MAMA, MRS. BREEDLOVE and MAUREEN] enter wearing large straw hats. They carry a basket of clothes [brown] and a line and clothes pins. They stand, backs to audience, spread out across stage. They tie the line up and begin hanging clothes. Each turns to profile when she talks. FRIEDA

and CLAUDIA move around them listening through the exchange.)

WOMAN 1. Girl, you heard 'bout the Breedloves?

FRIEDA. Seem like that's all people do is talk about other people.

WOMAN 2. Lord, if it's not one thing with them people it's another.

FRIEDA. Like they know what they sayin'.

WOMAN 3. What had happened?

WOMAN 1. Seem Cholly at it again. Went upside that woman's head, should have knocked her clean out her senses, but she got such a hard head.

WOMAN 2. Heard now they outdoors.

WOMAN 3. Outdoors?

WOMAN 1 & 2. Yes Lord, that's right, outdoors.

(WOMEN pause, mid hanging.)

CLAUDIA *(to audience)*. Outdoors was the real terror of life. If somebody ate too much, he could end up outdoors.

FRIEDA. If somebody used too much coal, he could end up outdoors.

CLAUDIA. People could gamble themselves outdoors...

FRIEDA. Drink themselves outdoors...

CLAUDIA. Sometimes mothers put their sons outdoors, and when that happened,

FRIEDA. No matter what the son had done,

CLAUDIA. All sympathy was with him.

WOMAN 1. Lord knows if we ever got put out, I would leave town for the embarrassment.

FRIEDA. But understand, there is a difference between being put *out* and being put out*doors*. If you are put out, you go somewhere else; if you are outdoors, there is no place to go.

WOMAN 2. Some people jes ain't got no pride.

WOMAN 3. I told Pete, he ever put me in a position like that, I like to die first.

WOMAN 1. Your Pete, my Avery, ain't none of them dippin' into the sauce enough for that to happen.

WOMAN 2. Lord know that's right.

WOMAN 1. So anyway, county got them split up, placed with families 'til it all get sorted out.

FRIEDA. So, county placed Pecola with us and she gone stay with us 'til they can reunite her family. That's what they say.

CLAUDIA. Well, whatever "they" had to say about it, we had fun in those days while Pecola was with us. Frieda and I stopped fighting each other and concentrated on helping our guest not feel outdoors.

(Fade to previous lighting.)

PECOLA. So it's just 'til Mrs. Breedlove, Mama, put up some wallpaper… She gone stay with the white people she work for.

(The WOMEN exit.)

CLAUDIA. Here, Pecola, you turn. *(Hands PECOLA the jump rope.)*

FRIEDA. That's not nice.

CLAUDIA. What?

FRIEDA. She's our guest.

CLAUDIA *(to PECOLA)*. Fine, then you can jump. *(PE-COLA tries to jump rope and fails.)* Try again. *(Still fails.)*

FRIEDA. Maybe I could get some graham crackers.

PECOLA. I don't care.

FRIEDA. I could get some graham crackers and milk. *(Beat.)* I have a Shirley Temple cup you can use, but you can't tell Mama because we supposed to take our snacks inside.

PECOLA. I love Shirley Temple.

CLAUDIA. Why?

PECOLA. I don't know. She's pretty and talented and people love her.

CLAUDIA. I don't.

PECOLA & FRIEDA. Why?

CLAUDIA. I don't know.

PECOLA. Did you see her in that movie where she danced with Bo Jangles?

CLAUDIA. That's why I hate her.

FRIEDA. Claudia just mad 'cause she want to dance with Bo Jangles.

(Light changes. PECOLA and FRIEDA continue playing. Game switches to a silent clapping game.)

CLAUDIA. So. *(To audience.)* Truth be told, what I felt for Shirley Temple was unsullied hatred. Mr. Jangles wasn't supposed to be dancing with that white girl. He was *my* friend, *my* uncle, *my* daddy. He should have been soft-shoeing it and chuckling with me. At least with someone who looked like me.

(FRIEDA and PECOLA produce dolls and begin playing with them.)

CLAUDIA *(cont'd)*. It all started with my annual blonde, blue-eyed Christmas doll. What was I supposed to do with it? Feed it? Rock it? Bathe it? Be its mother? *(Beat.)* I'll tell you what I did with it. I destroyed it. I had only one desire: to dismember it! If I could rip it apart, maybe I'd understand what the world thought was so wonderful about pink skin and yellow hair.

(CLAUDIA grabs PECOLA's doll from her. PECOLA fawns over FRIEDA's doll. They brush her hair, change her clothes, etc. While CLAUDIA uses her doll to demonstrate.)

CLAUDIA *(cont'd)*. I would not, could not love it. I fingered the face, picked the pearly teeth, traced the turned-up nose, poked the glassy blue eyeballs. I'd break off the tiny fingers, bend the flat feet, pull out the hair, twist the head around. The thing made one horrible sound.

PECOLA & FRIEDA. MAA-MA.

CLAUDIA. It sounded to me like the bleat of a dying lamb.

PECOLA & FRIEDA. MAA-MA.

CLAUDIA. I'd remove the cold and stupid eyeball. It would stare at me with one eye and still bleat.

PECOLA & FRIEDA. MAA-MA.

CLAUDIA. Take off the head, shake out the sawdust, crack the back against the floor, it would bleat,

PECOLA & FRIEDA. MAA-MA.

CLAUDIA. ...still. The gauze back would split, and I could see the disk with six holes, the secret of the sound. Just a little box with holes, still bleating...

PECOLA & FRIEDA. MAA-MA.

CLAUDIA. And Mama would say,

MAMA. You don't know how to take care of nothing. I never had a baby doll in my whole life. Used to cry my eyes out to have one of my own. Now you got one, a beautiful one, and you tear it all up? Girl, what's the matter with you?

CLAUDIA. What was worse—I wanted to commit a systematic dismembering of real little white girls to understand what magic it was that they weaved on others. What made people look at them and say "Awwww," but not see me at all? Why was I invisible next to little white girls in pleated skirts and white knee-highs? If I pinched them *they* actually cried. Later I learned that my desire to harm white girls was repulsive. I substituted love for the pangs of guilt I could not bring myself to feel. So, I learned to make a show of "loving" Shirley Temple. I even convinced myself. But I was years away from understanding the complexity of my emotions and so was resigned to sit and fume while Frieda and Pecola played with their dolls on into the night.

(Lights fade on PECOLA, CLAUDIA and FRIEDA. FRIEDA and PECOLA coo over the baby, while CLAUDIA jumps rope by herself. The sound of the rope creates a rhythm that is picked up by MRS. BREED-LOVE's song.)

Scene vi

(MRS. BREEDLOVE enters and sings "Precious Lord..." It is soulful and beautiful.)

MRS. BREEDLOVE.
> *Precious Lord, take my hand*
> *Lead me on, let me stand*
> *I am tired, I am weak, I am worn,*

(MRS. BREEDLOVE continues singing. PECOLA enters and reads from the primer.)

PECOLA. See Mother. Mother is very nice. Mother, will you play a game with Jane?

(CLAUDIA enters. PECOLA watches.)

MRS. BREEDLOVE.
> *Through the storms, through the night*
> *Lead me on to the light*
> *Take my hand, precious Lord, lead me on.*

CLAUDIA. When Pecola's mama, Mrs. Breedlove, was two, she stepped on a rusty nail that went clean through her foot. From then on she had a kind of flippity floppity limp that distinguished her from others, and also gave her something to pin all her misery on. That and the front tooth that rotted away and fell out later in life.

FRIEDA. Mrs. Breedlove was fifteen when the war ended, her family moved to Kentucky, in search of a better life.

CLAUDIA. To Mrs. Breedlove the change in location barely mattered. She still took care of her brothers and sisters, and so her world remained as small as three rooms, a patch of front yard, and the dusty path to church.

MRS. BREEDLOVE. Fantasies about men and love and touching were drawing my mind and hands away from my work. I would sit in church and dream of a man who would appear out of nowhere. He would carry in him tenderness, strength and a promise of rest. I would lay my head on his chest and he would lead me away to the sea, or the city, or the woods forever.

Precious Lord, take my hand
Lead me on, let me stand...

CLAUDIA. And then he did come.

(Light fades on PECOLA and CLAUDIA as CHOLLY enters, whistling "Precious Lord.")

MRS. BREEDLOVE. He came, strutting out of a Kentucky sun on the hottest day of the year. He came big, he came strong, he came with yellow eyes, flaring nostrils and he came with his own music. *(To CHOLLY:)* You whistle real pretty.

CHOLLY. Thank you. You real pretty yourself.

MRS. BREEDLOVE. No. *(Beat.)* I clean up awright I guess. *(Pause.)* You hungry?

CHOLLY. No ma'am. Just pickin' some berries for later.

MRS. BREEDLOVE. Me too. Maybe make a pie tonight.

CHOLLY. What happened to your foot?

MRS. BREEDLOVE. Accident.

CHOLLY. I didn't mean nothin' by it. Just makin' conversation. It don't hurt you, do it?

MRS. BREEDLOVE *(to CHOLLY)*. It only hurts sometimes when it rains, sometime.

CHOLLY. May I?

MRS. BREEDLOVE. And he knelt down on the dusty
ground and tickled my foot. Then he kissed my foot,
real soft. Then he was kissing my leg. And that's when I
knew Cholly Breedlove was the man I dreamed about in
church. That was the moment we first started loving
each other I imagine. He treated me real gentle. Made
me laugh. Made me his wife and took me North, away
from everything I had knowed. I didn't mind that he
sometimes drank too much, 'cause it seem like we was
all the time laughing. But I missed my people. Those
white folks in the North, seem like they was all over us,
and what few colored folks we did see was different too.
Dicty-like. No better than whites for meanness. That was
the lonesomeness time of my life. That put a lot of pres-
sure on Cholly to be my husband *and* my only friend in
the world both.

*(Lights fade and movie-screen effect plays across MRS.
BREEDLOVE's face.)*

CLAUDIA. Mrs. Breedlove found some comfort and company in the cinema.

FRIEDA. The cinema?

CLAUDIA. Movies, stupid.

MRS. BREEDLOVE *(cont'd)*. The onliest time I be happy
seem like was when I was in the picture show. They'd
cut off the lights, and everything be black. Then the
screen would light up, and I'd move right on in them
pictures. Gave me a lot of pleasure. But it made coming

home hard, and looking at Cholly even harder. I started to spend all my housekeeping money on clothes and some nice things for the house to be more like them happy white people in the pictures. Seem like Cholly was using all our money to drink more and more, and I steady looking at him like he nothin'.

CLAUDIA. On one day, not any less or more ugly than any of Mrs. Breedlove's days, she went to the cinema to see Clark Gable and Jean Harlow.

MRS. BREEDLOVE. I fixed my hair up like I'd seen hers on a magazine.

(FRIEDA stands behind her, hands her a hand mirror in which to primp, combing her hair.)

FRIEDA. A part on the side, with one little curl on the forehead.

MRS. BREEDLOVE. I thought it looked just like her.

FRIEDA. Well, almost just like.

CLAUDIA. Frieda!

MRS. BREEDLOVE. Anyway I was just sitting there, all in the picture, thinking I looked cute, when I bit down on a piece of candy and my front tooth comes clean out its socket. I could of cried. There I was, five months pregnant, trying to look like Jean Harlow, and my front tooth's gone. Didn't care no more after that. I settled down to being ugly, and goin' to them pictures just made me more ugly. Then Cholly started into makin' fun of the way I looked and that hurt me somethin' terrible. So, me and Cholly was fighting even more. I swear I tried to kill him, but he didn't hit me too hard, I guess 'cause I was pregnant. He used to make me madder than anything I knowed. I 'spect I made him mad too, and so that was just what our life looked like from then on.

(Blackout.)

Scene vii

(Light rises on MAMA, fussin'. In a separate area of the stage, PECOLA, FRIEDA and CLAUDIA sit.)

MAMA. Lord have mercy. Three quarts of milk. That's what was in that icebox yesterday. Three whole quarts. Now they ain't none. Not a drop. I don't mind folks coming in and getting what they want, but three quarts of milk! What the devil does *any*body need with *three* quarts of milk?

CLAUDIA. She talkin' 'bout Pecola.

FRIEDA. We knew that, Claudia, you didn't need to say it out loud.

CLAUDIA. Why you drink so much milk, Pecola?

PECOLA. I don't know.

FRIEDA. I do. It's 'cause you like using that Shirley Temple cup, ain't it?

PECOLA. Guess so. You think I ought to explain to your mama?

CLAUDIA & FRIEDA. No.

CLAUDIA. It'd just make her more mad.

MAMA. I don't know what I supposed to be running here. A charity ward I guess. Time for me to get out of the *giving* line and into the *getting* line. I guess I ain't supposed to have nothing. I'm supposed to end up in the

poorhouse. Folks just spend all their time trying to figure out ways to send *me* to the poorhouse. I got about as
much business with another mouth to feed as a cat has
with side pockets.

PECOLA. Cats don't have pockets.

FRIEDA. She just talkin'.

PECOLA. We gone get in trouble?

FRIEDA & CLAUDIA. No.

CLAUDIA. She just like to blow off steam is all. It don't
mean nothin'.

MAMA. There's a limit to everything. Don't nobody need
three quarts of milk, Henry Ford don't need three quarts
of milk. That's just downright sinful. This has got to
stop and I'm just the one to stop it. That old trifling
Cholly been out of jail two whole days and ain't been
here yet to see if his own child was 'live or dead. And
that mama neither. What kind of something is that?

*(Long pause. One of the girls examines a scrape under a
Band-aid, another slaps at a mosquito, while a third
makes lazy designs in the dirt with a stick. This goes on
for a long while. Finally:)*

FRIEDA. We better git 'fore she start in 'bout Roosevelt
and the CCC camps and…

FRIEDA, CLAUDIA & MAMA. "all them people who
don't care whether we got a loaf of bread."

MAMA. Think I'm some kind of Sandy Clause. Well they
can just take the stockings down 'cause it ain't Christmas.

FRIEDA. Let's do something.

CLAUDIA. Watchu wan' do?

FRIEDA. I don't know. Nothing.

(Same long pause as before.)

CLAUDIA. Want to go up and look at Daddy's dirty mag-
azines what he hides under the mattress?

FRIEDA. You know I don't like to look at them ugly pictures. You like to look at ugly pictures of naked people,
Pecola?

PECOLA. No, uh-uh. That ain't civ-lized.

CLAUDIA. Well, we could look at the Bible? That's
civ-lized. *(The girls remain silent. Clearly it's a bad
idea. Then:)* OK then. We could go thread needles for
the half-blind lady. She'll give us a penny.

FRIEDA. Her eyes look like snot. I don't feel like looking
at them.

CLAUDIA. We could go ask Soaphead Church to tell us
our futures.

*(Light rises on SOAPHEAD CHURCH. He stands on a
small crate, furiously polishing a teakettle.)*

FRIEDA. He a little scary. 'Sides, Daddy said stay away
from him.

CLAUDIA *(to audience)*. Soaphead was a true, profes-
sional fortuneteller and chirpretater of dreams.

FRIEDA. Inter-cher-per-a-tay-tor.

CLAUDIA. That's what I said! *(To PECOLA.)* She always
think she know something.

*(SOAPHEAD pockets the kettle and ceremoniously flour-
ishes his card.)*

SOAPHEAD CHURCH. Elihue Micah Whitcomb, aka Soaphead Church.

CLAUDIA. He talks smart and he even has is own business card.

SOAPHEAD CHURCH. Spritualist, Psychic Reader and Interpreter of Dreams. If you are unhappy, discouraged, or in distress, *(FRIEDA begins speaking, SOAPHEAD continues under her)* I can help you. Does bad luck seem to follow you? Has the one you loved changed? I can help. Questions of truth, honesty, faith, are deceit? I will reveal the truth…

FRIEDA. Only person we knew with a business card was the insurance man.

SOAPHEAD CHURCH. I will tell you who your enemies and friends are, and if the one you love is true or false.

PECOLA. I guess we could go by there.

FRIEDA. Uh-uh. 'Sides, look at me, I don't need ole Soaphead tell me I gone have a boyfriend one day.

CLAUDIA. Fine. I didn't want to go over to Soaphead's house anyway.

(SOAPHEAD pockets his card, turns his back and resumes his polishing as his light fades.)

CLAUDIA. But he does know stuff. Lots of stuff. *(Pause.)* Why don' you think what to do for change…

FRIEDA. Don't know…

CLAUDIA. Shoot then. What *you* want to do, Pecola?

PECOLA. I don't care.

CLAUDIA. We could go up the alley and see what's in the trash cans.

FRIEDA. Too cold.

CLAUDIA. We could make some fudge.

FRIEDA. You kidding, with Mama in there fussing at the walls, you know she's gonna be at it all day.

PECOLA. Seem like she wouldn't let us anyway.

CLAUDIA. Well, let's go over to the Greek hotel and listen to them cuss.

FRIEDA. They always say the same words. 'Sides that's unciv-lized too.

CLAUDIA *(to audience)*. It was at this moment that Pecola's world changed. The moment had only a peripheral effect on us, but Pecola's world would be forever altered. In that moment she was made more vulnerable than we could even imagine.

PECOLA. Oh my.

FRIEDA. What.

PECOLA. Ohhhh, I don't know what's happening.

CLAUDIA. You sick?

PECOLA. Maybe so. Must be. *(PECOLA begins to cry. She stands, and where she was sitting and down her legs, there is a small, but noticeable amount of blood.)*

CLAUDIA. Don't cry.

FRIEDA. Oh Lordy! I know what that is. *(Beat.)* You ministratin'!

PECOLA. I think I gone die! Will I die?

FRIEDA. Noo. You won't die. It just means you can have a baby.

PECOLA. What?

CLAUDIA. How you know? Always think you know everything. Like you the authority on ministratin'.

FRIEDA. Mama told me.

CLAUDIA. Don't make you queen of ministratin'.

FRIEDA. I know what to do. Claudia, you go and get some water to wash off the porch with. Pecola, stop crying and give me your drawers.

PECOLA. Take them off?

FRIEDA. It's the only way.

PECOLA. Whachu gone do with them? They's the only drawers I got.

FRIEDA. We'll bury them and you can have some I don't wear no more.

(Just as PECOLA has taken off her panties and is handing them to FRIEDA, MAMA enters.)

MAMA. Y'all come in now and get washed up. Got the hot water cornbread on so it'll only be a minute... Lord have mercy, what you all doin' here? On no, Claudia, get me a switch. I won't have my girls playin' nasty. I'd rather raise pigs then some nasty girls, least I can slaughter pigs. *(MAMA grabs FRIEDA by the arm and begins spanking her.)* I said go get me a switch! What, now you can't hear? These girls here playin' nasty and you deaf. Lord help us all.

CLAUDIA. No, Mama, that ain't how it is. She was bleeding. We was just tryin' to stop the blood.

FRIEDA. It's true, Mama. She was ministratin', like you told me about. We was just helping.

MAMA. All right, all right. Now stop cryin'. Mama didn't know. Come now. Git on in the house.

CLAUDIA. We trooped in. No longer in search of a meaningless distraction to help the day pass. That night as the three of us lay in bed,

FRIEDA. Me in my usual spot on the outside, Pecola in the middle,

CLAUDIA. And I'm against the wall, furthest away from anything that might lurk under the bed and snatch me up, I thought how Pecola was now different from us. Grown-up-like. She probably felt it too, but she did not lord it over us. After a long while she spoke very softly.

PECOLA. It true I can have a baby now?

FRIEDA. Sure you can.

PECOLA. But how?

FRIEDA. Somebody has to love you.

PECOLA. Oh. *(Long pause.)* How you do that?

CLAUDIA. What?

PECOLA. How do you get somebody to love you?

CLAUDIA *(to audience).* But Frieda was asleep, and I didn't know.

(Blackout. END OF ACT I.)

ACT II

Scene i

(Set elements reflect winter. FRIEDA and CLAUDIA appear in same dresses as before, only now they are blue. Note: PECOLA will always appear in her dingy white dress.)

CLAUDIA. In winter Daddy gives us strict instructions about which doors to keep closed or opened for proper distribution of heat.

DADDY. What you need to do is always keep the kitchen door propped open six inches or so...more than that you get a cold cross breeze, but you close it and there's no air to move the heat from the stove to the back rooms. What you need to do is...

CLAUDIA. He lays kindling by, discusses the qualities of coal, and instructs us on how best to care for the fire.

DADDY. No, baby girl, gently...you want to blow on the cinders, but gently...too hard you'll just stir up dirt and smoke, too soft, we'll lose the flame...

(FRIEDA enters with two pairs of dark blue stockings. PECOLA is with her, but stands to the side and watches the girls remove their fall stockings and pull on the winter ones.)

FRIEDA. In winter we put pepper in the feet of our stockings, Vaseline on our faces, and forced ourselves to swallow breakfasts of slippery lumps of cold oatmeal and cocoa with a roof of skin.

CLAUDIA. But mostly, we wait for spring when there will be gardens.

FRIEDA. But then, somewhere in the middle of the winter gloom, a distraction.

(With great musical fanfare, a bright white light reveals MAUREEN, beautifully coiffed and clothed in the same palette of blues, though her colors seem brighter, fresher, her fabrics more expensive. All three girls look at her, awestruck.)

CLAUDIA, FRIEDA & PECOLA. Maureen Peal.

PECOLA. She's *beautiful.*

CLAUDIA. She isn't all that.

FRIEDA. Is too.

CLAUDIA. Fine! *(To audience.)* OK. *(Beat.)* Maureen was beautiful. A high-yellow dream child with long brown hair braided in two lynch ropes that hung down her back.

PECOLA. I think she's rich.

CLAUDIA. Rich at least by our standards.

FRIEDA. She was as rich as the richest of the white girls.

CLAUDIA. The quality of her clothes threatened to derange us.

FRIEDA. There was a hint of spring in her sloe green eyes,

PECOLA. Her skin bright and yellow and smooth and soft like churned butter.

CLAUDIA. She enchanted the entire school. When teachers called on her they smiled encouragingly. Black boys didn't trip her in the halls; white boys didn't stone her,

FRIEDA. White girls didn't suck their teeth when she was assigned to be their work partners; black girls stepped aside when she wanted to use the sink in the girls' toilet.

PECOLA. She always has lunch money and never eats alone.

FRIEDA. She even likes white milk.

CLAUDIA. Frieda and I were both irritated and fascinated by her. We looked hard for flaws, but the most we could do was ugly up her name.

FRIEDA. Maureen Peal...Meringue Pie. Uh-huh. She nothin' but a big fat piece of nasty Meringue Pie.

CLAUDIA. We were overjoyed to learn that she had been born with six fingers on each hand and that there was a little bump where each extra one had been removed.

FRIEDA. And she had a dog tooth. A cute little thing, but a dog tooth nevertheless.

CLAUDIA. Six-finger-dog-tooth-meringue-pie. A small triumph to be sure. Behind the backs of her faithful and adoring public,

FRIEDA. Pecola included,

CLAUDIA. we snickered and called her names. Everything about her made us less. In her presence we became just a little bit dirtier, a little poorer, a bit more invisible, if that was possible even. And then, horror of horrors, she was assigned the locker next to mine.

(CLAUDIA moves to another area of the stage.)

MAUREEN. Hi.

CLAUDIA. Hi.

MAUREEN. Waiting for your sister?

CLAUDIA. Uh-huh.

MAUREEN. Which way do you go home?

CLAUDIA. Down Twenty-first Street to Broadway.

MAUREEN. Why don't you go down Twenty-second Street?

CLAUDIA. Because I live on Twenty-first Street.

MAUREEN. I guess I could walk part of the way that way.

CLAUDIA. Free country.

(FRIEDA and PECOLA enter.)

CLAUDIA. Maureen is going to walk part way with us.

MAUREEN. She stay at your house?

CLAUDIA. Her mama fixin' up their place.

MAUREEN. What's your name?

PECOLA. Pecola.

MAUREEN. My name is Maureen Peal. We just moved here.

CLAUDIA *(to audience)*. Of course we knew her name. Everyone knew her name.

MAUREEN. Pecola? Wasn't that the name of the girl in *Imitation of Life*?

PECOLA. What's that?

FRIEDA. A movie.

MAUREEN. The picture show, you know. Where this mulatto girl hates her mother 'cause she's black and ugly, but then she cries at the funeral. It was real sad. Everybody cries in it.

PECOLA. Oh.

MAUREEN. Anyway, when it comes back I'm going to see it again. My mother has seen it four times.

PECOLA. Mrs. Breed... My mama say she used to go to the show 'fore I was born.

MAUREEN. My mother told me that a girl where we used to live went to the beauty parlor and asked the lady to fix her hair like Hedy Lamarr's and the lady said, "Yeah, when you grow some hair like Hedy Lamarr's."

FRIEDA. Sounds crazy.

MAUREEN. She was. That girl was sixteen and didn't even start menstruating yet. Do you?

(The girls are silent. PECOLA raises her hand.)

MAUREEN. Me too. I started two months ago. My girl-friend in Toledo started before me and she thought she was dying.

PECOLA. You know what it's for?

MAUREEN. For babies. Babies need blood when they are inside of you, and if you are having a baby you don't menstruate, but when you're not you don't need the blood so it comes out.

PECOLA. How do the babies get the blood?

CLAUDIA. Everyone knows that.

FRIEDA. Then how?

CLAUDIA. Tell her, Maureen.

MAUREEN. Baby gets blood through the like-line. It's where your belly button is.

PECOLA. Then how come boys have belly buttons, they don't have babies?

CLAUDIA *(to audience)*. Seemed like a good question.

MAUREEN. I don't know. But I think boys have all sorts of things they don't need. Didn't you ever see a naked man?

PECOLA. No. Where would I see a naked man. That would be un-civlized.

MAUREEN. I don't know. I just asked the question.

PECOLA. I wouldn't even look at a naked man if he stood in front of me. That would be nasty. Who wants to see a naked man? Nobody's father would be naked in front of his own daughter. Not unless he was dirty too.

MAUREEN. I didn't say anything about father. I just said a naked man.

PECOLA. Oh, well I thought…

MAUREEN. How come you said "father"?

CLAUDIA. Who else would she see, dog tooth? (To audience.) I was glad for a real reason to be mad. Truth be told, I was a little jealous that Maureen turned all her sunshine attention on Pecola. Like they were best friends or something.

MAUREEN. I wasn't talking to you anyway. I don't care if she sees her father naked all day and all night. Who cares?

FRIEDA. You do because you have a dirty mind.

MAUREEN. Is not.

FRIEDA. Is too. Boys, babies, and somebody's naked daddy. You crazy.

MAUREEN. You better be quiet.

FRIEDA. You gone make me?

MAUREEN. You already made. Mammy made.

CLAUDIA. You better not be talkin' 'bout our mama.

MAUREEN. You stop talking about my daddy.

FRIEDA. Who said anything about your daddy?

MAUREEN. You did.

CLAUDIA. Well you started it.

MAUREEN. I wasn't talking to either of you. I was talking to Pecola.

CLAUDIA. 'Bout seeing her daddy naked.

MAUREEN. So what if she did see him?

PECOLA. I never saw my daddy naked. Never.

MAUREEN. Did too. All the kids say so. Say you a daddysleepnekked black-ee-mo.

PECOLA. I did not.

MAUREEN. Did. Your own daddy too! I've never heard of anything so nasty.

(PECOLA pulls in on herself. The same stance we saw at the top of play.)

CLAUDIA. Stop talking about her daddy.

MAUREEN. What do I care about her old black daddy?

CLAUDIA. Oh no she didn't.

FRIEDA. Oh yes she did.

CLAUDIA. Who are you calling black?

MAUREEN. You.

CLAUDIA. You think you're so cute.

(CLAUDIA swings, but misses and accidentally hits PECOLA. FRIEDA joins the fray, PECOLA simply stands, near tears. MAUREEN puts up a good fight and manages to run away. Chase takes place through the house.)

MAUREEN. I am cute. And you are ugly. All of you are ugly ugly black-eee-mos. I *am* cute.

CLAUDIA & FRIEDA. Six-finger-dog-tooth-meringue-pie. Six-finger-dog-tooth-meringue-pie. Six-finger-dog-tooth-meringue-pie.

(MAUREEN is gone. Long moment of silence.)

PECOLA. She sure is pretty, donchu think.

(Light fades.)

Scene ii

(PECOLA reads as MRS. BREEDLOVE enters.)

CLAUDIA. Before Cholly was Pecola's daddy, and Mrs. Breedlove's husband,

SOAPHEAD CHURCH. he was a little baby what was left by his mama on a junk heap.

PECOLA. See Father. He is big and strong. Father, will you play with Jane?

CHOLLY. 'Bout all Aunt Jimmy would tell me 'bout my daddy was he didn't stay 'round long enough to see Mama's stomach get big with me. *(Beat.)* Hard to say how my life with Aunt Jimmy was. Seems like you just take life as it comes when you're up in the middle of it. I do recollect sometimes when I be watching Aunt Jimmy cross the table, eating collard greens with her fingers or sucking on her gold teeth, I would wonder if it might have been just as well if I had died there on that junk heap. Even so, she was the closest thing I ever had to a mother.

(Women cast members enter. They wear black dresses and hats. Their faces covered with black veils. They cross in front of the table and help CHOLLY into a suit jacket and tie while he speaks.)

SOAPHEAD CHURCH. Jimmy's funeral was Cholly's first. The ladies gathered around him, treating him like the child he never was.

CHOLLY. It was spring in my fifteenth year when Aunt Jimmy died. I got a new dark suit, white shirt and tie. Hot meals came in baskets covered with cheesecloth. The house was cleaned and a white outfit that looked like a wedding dress was made for Aunt Jimmy to meet Jesus in.

(The ladies sew a long piece of lacy white fabric. Sometimes they pull or bite the thread in unison. Sometimes their sewing is sporadic and frantic.)

WOMAN 1. What'd she die from?

WOMAN 2. Essie's peach pie.

WOMAN 3. Don't say.

WOMAN 2. Yes ma'am.

WOMAN 3. You know, m'dear, the medicine woman told her not to eat anything but pot liquor 'til the fever let up.

WOMAN 2. So, Jimmy ate every kind of pot liquor. Think she was almost better.

WOMAN 3. But that pie did her in.

WOMAN 1. Essie must feel mighty bad.

WOMAN 2. Oh, Lord, yes. But I told her, the Lord giveth and the Lord taketh away. Wasn't her fault none.

WOMAN 3. She makes good peach pies. But she bound to believe it was the pie did it, and I 'spect she right.

WOMAN 2. I 'spect so.

WOMAN 1. 'Spect so.

WOMAN 1, 2 & 3. 'Spect so. *(Women stop sewing, needles in air. Beat. Women resume sewing.)*

WOMAN 3. Did she leave anything?

WOMAN 1. Not even a pocket handkerchief. The house belongs to some white folks in Clarksville.

WOMAN 2. I hear the insurance folks been down talking to her brother.

WOMAN 3. How much do it come to?

WOMAN 1. Eighty-five dollars and something.

WOMAN 3. That all?

WOMAN 1. Can she get in the ground on that?

WOMAN 2. Don't see how.

WOMAN 1. Seem a shame. She been paying on that insurance all her life.

WOMAN 3. Don't I know.

WOMAN 2. Um-huh.

WOMAN 1. Yes sir.

(Pause. The women stop sewing, bite the thread, rethread needles, and resume sewing.)

CLAUDIA. The women chattered far into the night. Their creamy conversation made Cholly lean in, the words filling him with sadness. Still he did not cry.

WOMAN 3. What about the boy? What he gone do?

WOMAN 2. Cain't nobody find his mama.

WOMAN 1. Everybody sure liked old Jimmy. Sure will miss her.

WOMAN 2 & 3. Yes sir.
WOMAN 1. She will be missed.
WOMAN 2. That she will.

(The women lay the cloth [Jimmy] on a table. We are now in church.)

SOAPHEAD CHURCH. Still, he did not cry. Instead he sat on the floor in a corner of the room, watching the ladies' hems and men's polished work boots dance a social jig he did not entirely understand.
CHOLLY. It did not seem like Aunt Jimmy was really dead. Everything had happened so fast. It was more interesting than sad. When it was my turn to view the body I reached out my hand to touch Aunt Jimmy. But I couldn't bring myself to. She just looked too private.

(DARLENE enters.)

DARLENE. Hi, Cholly.
CHOLLY. Hi, Darlene.
DARLENE. She look like she sleep.
CHOLLY. Yeah, guess she do.
DARLENE. My grandma died last summer and when I touched her cheek it felt like wax.
CHOLLY. Oh.
DARLENE. Yeah. Mama says to be nice to you 'cause you all alone in the world.
CHOLLY. Guess so.
DARLENE. You sad?
CHOLLY. Maybe.
DARLENE. Why ainchu cryin'?

CHOLLY. Too old.

DARLENE. If it was my auntie, I'd be cryin' somethin' awful.

CHOLLY. That's 'cause you a girl.

DARLENE. I am. *(Long pause.)* You want maybe to come with me and pick muscadine?

CHOLLY. Don't know if they ripe yet.

DARLENE. Won't matter. 'Sides, I like it when they kind of tart, just before they ripe. Make your teeth stand on edge.

CLAUDIA. And so it was that young Cholly's melancholy was replaced for the moment with the promise of something daring and new.

(They exit.)

Scene iii

(In V.O. we hear children playing on a playground. PECOLA sits center stage reading.)

PECOLA. Who will play. Who will play with Jane. *(She closes the book, speaks to audience.)* Sometimes, when I get all the folding and ironing done for Mrs. Breedlove, I go on a candy adventure.

(CLAUDIA enters.)

CLAUDIA. Seem like a simple enough thing. Only nothin' simple for Pecola Breedlove.

(PECOLA enters her own light downstage.)

PECOLA. I walk down Garden Avenue. I mostly look at things on the sidewalk and wonder. I wonder why pretty yellow dandelions is called weeds. I like them. They strong and grow fast and don't hurt no one. When I look hard enough I sometime find a penny. When I have three, I put them in my shoe. This sidewalk a good one for skating. I don't have skates, but I think because it is old and smooth, the skates would go over it real nice. There's a crack shaped like a Y that I trip over most of the time. The ants go into that crack and I think they must have a whole world under there that makes some kind of sense to them.

CLAUDIA. Pecola pulls off her shoe, takes out the three pennies and climbs the four wooden steps to the door of Yacobowski's Fresh Vegetables Meat & Sundries Stoor. *(A bell tinkles when she opens the door.)* Mr. Yacobowski stands behind the counter and looks but doesn't really see Pecola.

PECOLA. Hello, Mr. Yacobowski. *(Beat.)* He doesn't say nothin' to me. Like he can't even hear me.

CLAUDIA. It's a total absence of human recognition, a glazed separateness right behind his eyes. Pecola has seen interest, disgust, even anger in grown male eyes. But this vacuum has an edge. An edge of distaste that lurks in the eyes of all white people. The distaste is for her blackness, because what else could it be, is right there, in his bottom eyelid. Pecola points, leaving a little smudge on the glass counter, utters a timid:

PECOLA. Three Mary Janes please… *(Opens her hand to reveal the three pennies.)* Mr. Yacobowski don't want to touch my hand. Finally…

CLAUDIA. The exchange is made.

PECOLA. Three perfect yellow rectangles.

CLAUDIA. The brief predictable moment of humiliation is replaced by the promise of something sweet.

(Light fades.)

Scene iv

(DARLENE and CHOLLY enter. Time has elapsed. They are slightly more rumpled, their pails now full of grapes.)

SOAPHEAD CHURCH. The way to the wild muscadine vineyard was through several backyards, across an open field, and through a dried riverbed. The little green going-to-purple grapes were too new and tight to have much sugar in them, but Cholly liked to eat them anyway. And on this day, the promise of sweetness that had yet to unfold excited them both more than full ripeness would have.

CLAUDIA. That was years before Cholly made Pecola's mama Mrs. Breedlove, that was years before anybody went upside anybody's head, and anybody was put out of anywhere. That was years before the seeds did not grow. Maybe it's when it all started to go terribly wrong.

(DARLENE and CHOLLY enter from R. Time has elapsed. They are slightly more rumpled, their pails now full.)

DARLENE. Watchu gone do now?

CHOLLY. Don't know. Just wander 'round I guess, maybe look for my daddy.

DARLENE. You know where he at?

CHOLLY. Don't even know who he is. Aunt Jimmy once told me his name. Thought I might look 'round Macon. Probaly won't find him. *(Beat.)* You want some more grapes?

DARLENE. Naw. We gone need to get back soon. My mama'll whip me if I come back late. Might whip me anyway 'cause my dress all messed up.

SOAPHEAD CHURCH. The sun had gone. The smell of promised rain, pine and muscadine made Cholly giddy. Turning his head to see where the moon was, Cholly caught sight of Darlene, huddled into a "D."

(DARLENE struggles with the bow that has come undone in her hair.)

DARLENE. Yeah, Mama gone whup me for sure, I'm all messed up.

SOAPHEAD CHURCH. A new emotion caught Cholly off guard. His giddiness was replaced with an emptiness. He had finally realized that Aunt Jimmy was dead and the sudden absence of someone to whup him took his breath away.

CHOLLY. You don't look so bad to me. Let me help.

(CHOLLY rises to his knees, facing her, and attempts to help tie her ribbon. A blue wash turns their white clothes to a dark purple. The moment is about to become a kiss. They freeze. A cello plays "Precious Lord.")

CLAUDIA. They came together as natural and sweet as the night the day had become. It was at once playful and exciting.

SOAPHEAD CHURCH. The act itself was not as difficult as Cholly had imagined it would be and felt more like home than anything he had ever known. As his own excitement grew he heard her moans as no more than the pines sighing above his head.

(DARLENE screams, the light on the two of them goes to black. We see them in splashes of white light. They react to the men who we do not see.)

SOAPHEAD CHURCH. He thought he had hurt her until he saw her face staring wildly at something over his shoulder. He jerked around.

CHOLLY. There stood two white men. One with a spirit lamp and one with a flashlight.

DARLENE. No mistaking they were white.

CHOLLY. You could smell it on them.

(CHOLLY stands in front of DARLENE, staring straight out, attempting to shield his eyes. The sound of the white men's voices is muffled and stylized, the words barely audible, the meaning clear.)

SOAPHEAD CHURCH *(as MAN 1)*. Get on wid it.

CHOLLY. Sir?

SOAPHEAD CHURCH *(as MAN 1)*. I said, get on wid it. And make it good. Make it real good. *(They laugh.)*

SOAPHEAD CHURCH. There was no place for Cholly's eyes to go. He was paralyzed. The white man lifted his gun down from his shoulder. Cholly heard the clop of metal. *(Sound effect.)* He dropped back to his knees.

DARLENE. Darlene held onto Cholly and stared out of the lamplight into the darkness, looking almost unconcerned, as though they had no part in the drama taking place around them.

CHOLLY. Her hands clutching his wrist looked like claws.

SOAPHEAD CHURCH. With a violence born of total helplessness, Cholly pulled up her dress and lowered his trousers and underwear.

SOAPHEAD CHURCH *(as MAN 2)*. That's right, go on now.

SOAPHEAD CHURCH. Darlene put her hands over her face as Cholly began to simulate what had before been beautiful and was now something ugly and confusing. He could do no more than make believe. And he hated her for it. Hated her so much he almost wished he could do it.

CHOLLY. He almost wished he could hurt her to make up for the hurt and shame he felt.

SOAPHEAD CHURCH *(as MAN 1)*. Hurry it up, boy. We got to be goin', don't have all day.

SOAPHEAD CHURCH *(as MAN 2)*. Come on... They be lookin' for us.

(We hear dogs in the distance, blackout. All is silence. When the natural light returns, CHOLLY and DARLENE

*are standing, adjusting clothes, not looking at one an-
other.)*

CHOLLY. We best be gettin' back.
DARLENE. Yes. Best we do.

(They exit. Light fades.)

Scene v

(Lights rise on PECOLA.)

PECOLA. I take the same sidewalk, past the same crack.
Past the same dandelions. Come to think of it, maybe
they are weeds. Yes, they are ugly. Ugly weeds. Nobody
would think a weed is pretty. You would have to be stupid to think a weed is pretty. *(She stomps on the dande-
lion, crushing it into the ground.)* I sit on the edge of the
empty playground. I like the playground when it is
empty. It is safe and quiet. Before I eat my Mary Janes,
I look at each one. Each pretty little girl. Each girl's
name is Mary Jane and she has blonde curls and big
blue eyes. And she looks at me with those pretty eyes
and she is my friend. She has a treat for me. A peanut
butter treat that will last for a long time on my tongue
and will be just mine. I eat the candy, and it is almost
like I am Mary Jane. Lovely, lovely Mary Jane. Beautiful, happy Mary Jane.

(Light fades. END OF ACT II)

ACT III

Scene i

MRS. BREEDLOVE.
>   *Through the storms, through the night*
>   *Lead me on to the light*
>   *Take my hand, precious Lord, lead me on.*

(CLAUDIA enters. She and FRIEDA now are attired for spring. They wear crisp white dresses and shoes and stockings with light pastel accents. CLAUDIA sits, cross-legged, fingering a long sprig of yellow flowered pussy willow.)

CLAUDIA. The first twigs are thin, green, and supple. They bend into a complete circle but will not break. Their delicate, showy hopefulness shooting from forsythia and lilac bushes meant only a change in whipping style.

FRIEDA. Mama and Daddy beat us differently in the spring.

CLAUDIA. Instead of the dull pain of a winter strap, there were these new green switches that lost their sting long after the whipping was over.

FRIEDA. Only thing worse than Forsythia switches is castor oil.

CLAUDIA. Sunk in the grass of an empty lot on a spring Saturday, I split the stems of milkweed and think about ants and peach pits and death and where the world went when I closed my eyes. I must have sat there for a long time, because the shadow that was in front of the house when I left for my field has disappeared when I go back.

(Lights rise on CLAUDIA and FRIEDA approaching PE-COLA's house.)

FRIEDA. Whatchu wanna do today?

CLAUDIA. Not sure.

FRIEDA. We could have Soaphead see if you gone get a boyfriend...

CLAUDIA. We'd get skinned alive. Ain't worth it. Why don't we go cross town and see if Pecola's at her mama's work.

FRIEDA. Why you wan' go way over there?

CLAUDIA. Somethin' to do, I guess. Truth was, I missed Pecola. Since she had gone back to her house and school was now over, Frieda and I were bouncing off each other and the walls.

FRIEDA *(to audience)*. We decided to make the long walk cross town all the way to Lake Shore Park. Lake Shore Park was a glorious city park laid out with rosebuds, fountains, bowling greens, and picnic tables.

CLAUDIA. Black people were not allowed in the park and so it filled our dreams.

FRIEDA. Next to the entrance of the park was the large white house with the wheelbarrow full of flowers where Mrs. Breedlove worked. Pecola sat on a tiny stoop on the side of the house.

PECOLA. Hi.

CLAUDIA & FRIEDA. Hi.

PECOLA. What you all doing here?

CLAUDIA. Looking for you.

PECOLA. Who told you I was here?

FRIEDA. Where else you gone be?

CLAUDIA. You got time to come over to our house?

PECOLA. Mrs. Breedlove don't like me leaving far from here when I'm supposed to be helping.

(MRS. BREEDLOVE sticks her head out of the door. She's wearing her uniform.)

MRS. BREEDLOVE. What's going on here? Pecola, who are these children?

PECOLA. Mrs. MacTeer's girls, ma'am.

MRS. BREEDLOVE. What are you girls doing all the way over here?

CLAUDIA. Just walking.

FRIEDA. Came to see Pecola.

MRS. BREEDLOVE. She gone carry the wash home. Come in and wait while I get it.

(The girls enter a kitchen area, where a large pie sits on a table next to a large vase full of yellow flowers.)

CLAUDIA. We were led into a massive sparkling white kitchen. Odors of meat, vegetables, and something freshly baked filled the air.

MRS. BREEDLOVE. You all stand stock still right there and don't mess up nothing 'til I get back. *(Exits.)*

CLAUDIA. We hadn't had time to admire the fairy-book kitchen properly when another door opened and a little white girl walked in. If her hair wasn't long and straight and blonde and her eyes blue instead of green, I might have mistaken her for Shirley Temple.

(The little white GIRL is either represented by a white, life-sized doll, manipulated by the actress who plays MAUREEN PEAL, wearing an identical outfit, or the door opens to reveal a doll, and her lines are in V.O. The little GIRL wears pink sundress and pink fluffy bunny bedroom slippers.)

GIRL *(afraid)*. Where's Polly?
CLAUDIA. And there was my urge to squash her and perform the same ritual I performed on my white dolls. How could she call Mrs. Breedlove Polly? Mrs. Breedlove who was Mrs. Breedlove even to Pecola. *(To GIRL.)* She went downstairs to get the wash.
GIRL *(not moving)*. Polly. POLLY!

(FREIDA has been inching toward the pie.)

FRIEDA. Claudia. Pecola. Look at this.
GIRL. POLLY! Come here!
FRIEDA. This is the prettiest pie I've ever seen.
PECOLA. Me too. Mrs. Breedlove don't make things like this for us.
FRIEDA. I think it's still hot.

(PECOLA reaches out her hand to touch the pie as the little GIRL shrieks…)

GIRL. POLLLLYYYY!

(PECOLA is startled and knocks the pie off of table, they all freeze.)

CLAUDIA. That pie fell to the floor and splattered scalding hot blueberries everywhere. Most of the juice splashed up on Pecola's legs. Mrs. Breedlove returned faster than I would have thought she could move on that clubfoot. She was on top of Pecola in a heartbeat.

MRS. BREEDLOVE *(slaps PECOLA)*. Crazy fool...my floor, messed up. Look at what you did. Oh my floor, my floor... My floor. *(The GIRL begins to cry. MRS. BREEDLOVE picks up the doll.)* Oh baby. Hush hush. Hush now. Oh Lord, look at your pretty dress. Don't cry no more. Polly will change it. We'll have you in a pretty new dress in no time. *(To PECOLA.)* Pick up that wash and get on out of here so I can get this mess cleaned up.

GIRL. Who were they, Polly?

MRS. BREEDLOVE. Don't you worry none, baby.

GIRL. You gone make me another pie?

MRS. BREEDLOVE. Of course I will.

GIRL. But who were they?

MRS. BREEDLOVE. They weren't nobody. Hush now, don't you worry none.

CLAUDIA *(to audience)*. The honey in her words complimented the sundown spilling onto the lake and we all felt this as we began the long trek around the perimeter of the park toward home.

Scene ii

(A jazz riff of a very stylized, syncopated version of a hardly recognized "Precious Lord" plays under the following.

Each actor enters while speaking and stands on a different part of the stage.)

CLAUDIA. The pieces of Cholly's life could make sense only in the head of a musician.

SOAPHEAD CHURCH. Only a musician would have the tools to talk their talk through the gold of curved metal, or in the touch of black-and-white rectangles and taut skins and strings echoing from wooden corridors. Only a musician could give true form to Cholly's painful and confused life. Only they would know how to connect the tar black of a tire on a junk heap, the funky purple of muscadine, to the white of a flashlight on a boy's naked behind and come up with what all of that meant in joy, in pain, in anger, in love, and give it its final and pervading ache of freedom.

CLAUDIA. Only a musician would know, without even knowing what Cholly knew. That he was free. Not a good kind of freedom. A freedom tilting into madness born of the kind of loneliness and desperation that answers to no one. This kind of perverted freedom rendered him free to feel whatever he felt—

SOAPHEAD CHURCH. Free to be tender or violent, to whistle or weep.

CHOLLY. Free to take a job, free to leave it.

CLAUDIA. For who cared if he or his family was fed?

CHOLLY. Free to go to jail and not feel imprisoned…

CLAUDIA. For where better was there for him to be.

SOAPHEAD CHURCH. Free to smile and say to his jailer,

CHOLLY. I'm OK, sir.

SOAPHEAD CHURCH. For he had already killed three white men.

CHOLLY. Free to take a woman's insults,

MRS. BREEDLOVE. For his body had already conquered hers.

CHOLLY. Free even to knock her in the head.

SOAPHEAD CHURCH. For in his disturbed mind that right was his—

MRS. BREEDLOVE. because he had already cradled that head in his arms.

SOAPHEAD CHURCH. He was painfully free to drink himself into silly helplessness,

CHOLLY. For he had already been a gandy dancer, done thirty days on a chain gang, and picked a woman's bullet out of his own calf.

SOAPHEAD CHURCH. Free to live his own fantasies.

CHOLLY. Free even to die.

MRS. BREEDLOVE. It was with this freeness that he met, and married and loved Pauline Williams and turned her into Mrs. Breedlove.

CHOLLY. When he saw her, leaning on a fence scratching herself with a broken foot,

MRS. BREEDLOVE. He fell in love and made her his.

SOAPHEAD CHURCH. And so it was on a Saturday afternoon that Cholly came home, wrapped in this warped sense of freedom, staggering in the thin light of spring, reeling drunk,

CHOLLY. that he saw his daughter in the kitchen.

(Light comes up on PECOLA. She stands with her back to the audience.

CHOLLY makes his way toward her.)

PECOLA. She was washing dishes.

SOAPHEAD CHURCH. Her small back hunched over the sink.

CHOLLY. Cholly saw her dimly and could not tell what he saw or what he felt. He became aware that he was uncomfortable; but then, like so many times before, his uncomfortableness started to feel like pleasure. Then revulsion. Then guilt. Then pity. Then love.

SOAPHEAD CHURCH. Maybe not the kind of love found in the warm places, inhabiting the sweet spaces we all know, but the only kind of love Cholly had ever known. A violent, painful, lonely love. His revulsion was a reaction to her young, helpless, hopeless presence.

CHOLLY. She was just a child, why wasn't she happy? *(Beat.)* He wanted to break her neck.

SOAPHEAD CHURCH. But tenderly.

CHOLLY. Why did she have to look so whipped? What could he do for her—ever? What could he give to her? What could he say to her? What could a burned-out black man say to the hunched back of his eleven-year-old daughter? If he looked into her face, he would see those haunted, loving eyes.

SOAPHEAD CHURCH. The hauntedness would irritate him, the love would make him feel *(beat)* unworthy. His hatred of her slimed in his stomach and threatened to become vomit.

CHOLLY. But just before the puke moved into his mouth,

PECOLA. She shifted her weight and stood on one foot, scratching the back of her calf with her toe.

SOAPHEAD CHURCH. It was a quiet, familiar, and pitiful gesture. The timid, tucked-in look of the scratching toe—

CHOLLY. That was what Pauline was doing the first time he had seen her in Kentucky.

SOAPHEAD CHURCH. Leaning on that fence staring at nothing in particular.

CHOLLY. The creamy toe of her bare foot scratching a velvet leg.

ALL. It was such a simple gesture.

(In the following sequence CHOLLY joins PECOLA, whose back is to us the whole time. The two stand, never touching or moving.)

SOAPHEAD CHURCH. And once again, the dangerous, ugly, violent freedom. The desperate aching freedom to claim manhood through the most unspeakable…

CLAUDIA. Unthinkable…

CHOLLY. He sank to his knees, his eyes on Pecola's foot. Crawling on all fours toward her, he raised his hand and caught the foot in an upward stroke.

PECOLA. Pecola lost her balance and was about to careen to the floor.

CHOLLY. When Cholly raised his other hand to her hips to save her from falling. He put his head down and nibbled at the back of her leg. He closed his eyes, letting his fingers dig into her waist. The rigidness of her shocked body, the silence of stunned throat was better than Pauline's easy laughter had been.

SOAPHEAD CHURCH. The drunken, confused mixture of his memories of Pauline and the doing of a wild and forbidden thing excited him.

CHOLLY. No matter it was wrong.

SOAPHEAD CHURCH. For what was wrong to Cholly? Even if he had the power to discern wrong from right, it wouldn't matter for he lived only in the want of it.

CHOLLY. The next thing he knew, or maybe remembered, or maybe it didn't happen at all…

SOAPHEAD CHURCH. It happened.

CLAUDIA. It happened.

PECOLA. It happened.

CHOLLY. The next thing he remembered was her soapy hands on his wrists, the tiny fingers clenched tightly, like claws.

SOAPHEAD CHURCH. He removed himself from her small, dry, wounded body.

ALL WOMEN EXCEPT PECOLA. She seemed to have fainted.

CHOLLY. Cholly stood up. Once again the hatred mixed with tenderness. The hatred would not let him pick her up, the tenderness forced him to cover her. *(CHOLLY covers her and exits.)*

MRS. BREEDLOVE. So when the child regained consciousness, she was lying on the kitchen floor,

PECOLA. Trying to connect the pain with the face of Mrs. Breedlove floating over her.

(PECOLA sits up. We see her face for the first time as lights fade.)

CLAUDIA. So that is the ugly, untidy how of it. The why of it we continue to muddle through.

(Blackout.)

Scene iii

(It is summer. CLAUDIA and FRIEDA's dresses are grass green.)

FRIEDA. We have only to break into the tightness of a strawberry to know that it is summer.

CLAUDIA. Summer remains for me a season of storms. The parched days and sticky nights are undistinguished in my mind. But the storms, the violent sudden storms, both frightened and quenched me. The summer was already thick when Frieda and I received the seeds we had ordered.

FRIEDA. We had waited since April for the magic packets of seeds we would sell for five cents each.

CLAUDIA. The fastest, surest way to a new bicycle.

FRIEDA. We spent a major part of every day trooping around town selling them.

CLAUDIA. During that summer of seed selling we thought about the money, thought about the seeds, and listened with half an ear to what people were saying. Little by little we began to piece a story together, a secret, terrible, awful story. And it was only after two or three such vaguely overheard conversations that we realized the story was about Pecola.

(Three WOMEN come out with glasses of lemonade. They wear black hats like the ones worn in the funeral scene. They wear green.)

WOMAN 1. Did you hear about that girl?

WOMAN 2. What?

WOMAN 3. Pregnant?

WOMAN 1 & 2. Yesss.

WOMAN 1. But that's not all. Guess who?

(They all take a sip of lemonade.)

WOMAN 3. Who? I don't know all these little nappy-headed boys runnin' around here.

WOMAN 1. That's just it.

WOMAN 2. Ain't no little boy.

WOMAN 1. They say it's Cholly.

WOMAN 3. Cholly?

WOMAN 2. The girl's daddy!

WOMAN 1. Uh-huh.

WOMAN 3. Lord have mercy.

WOMAN 1. Nasty fool.

WOMAN 2. What's her mama gone do?

WOMAN 3. Keep on like she been, I reckon.

WOMAN 1. Heard he taken off.

WOMAN 3. County ain't gone keep that baby, is they?

(They all take a sip.)

WOMAN 1. Don't know.

WOMAN 2. None of them Breedloves seem right anyhow.

WOMAN 3. From your mouth to God's ears.

WOMAN 2. Whatchu reckon make him do a thing like that.

WOMAN 1. Beats me. Just nasty.

(They all take several long gulps, draining their cups.)

WOMAN 3. I do think this about the best lemonade I ever had.

WOMAN 2. Yes it is.

WOMAN 1. They ought to take her out of school.

WOMAN 2. Ought to.

WOMAN 3. She carry some of the blame.

WOMAN 1. She ain't but twelve or so.

WOMAN 2. Yeah, but you never know. How come she didn't fight him?

WOMAN 3. Maybe she did.

WOMAN 2. Yeah, you never know.

WOMAN 1. Well, it probably won't live.

WOMAN 2. They say the way her mama beat her, she lucky to be alive herself.

WOMAN 3. She lucky if id don't stay live.

WOMAN 1. Bound to be the ugliest thing walking.

WOMAN 2. Can't help but be. Ought to be a law: two ugly people doubling up like that to make more ugly. Be better off in the ground.

WOMAN 3. Margaret, you have any more this lemonade?

WOMAN 1. I could use some ice with it.

WOMAN 2. And that mint complemented it real nice.

(They all exit. CLAUDIA and FRIEDA remain.)

CLAUDIA. I thought about that baby that everybody wanted dead, and saw it very clearly. It was a dark, wet place, its head covered with great o's of wool, the black face holding, like nickels, two clean black eyes, the flared nose, kissing-thick lips, and the living, breathing silk of black skin. I felt a need for someone to want the black baby to live—just to counteract the universe of white baby dolls, Shirley Temples, and Maureen Peals.

FRIEDA. We wanted to do something to change the course of events and alter a human life.

CLAUDIA. What we gone do, Frieda?

FRIEDA. Ms. Johnson said it'd be a miracle if it lived.

CLAUDIA. So let's make it a miracle.

FRIEDA. How we gone do that? We cain't even make enough money for a bicycle.

CLAUDIA. We could pray.

FRIEDA. That's not enough. Remember the last time with the bird?

CLAUDIA. That was different, it was half dead when we found it.

FRIEDA. I don't care. We have to do something.

CLAUDIA. We could ask Him to let Pecola's baby live and promise to be good for a whole month.

FRIEDA. We better give up something so He'll know we really mean it this time.

CLAUDIA. We ain't got nothin' but two dollars in seed money.

FRIEDA. We could give that. Or know what? We could give up the bicycle. Bury the money and plant the seeds.

CLAUDIA. All the money?

FRIEDA. Claudia, you want to do it or donchu?

CLAUDIA. OK. I just thought...OK.

(FRIEDA begins digging. They strike the same pose they had when we met them at the top of the play. FRIEDA, on her knees, CLAUDIA standing behind her.)

FRIEDA. We have to do it right now. We'll bury the money over by her house so we can't go back and dig it up, and we'll plant the seeds here so we can watch over them. And when they come up, we'll know everything is all right. All right?

CLAUDIA. All right. Only let me sing this time. You say the magic words.

(CLAUDIA begins to sing "Precious Lord," and FRIEDA prays under her breath.)

Scene iv

(PECOLA enters. Reads from book.)

PECOLA. See the dog. Bow-wow-wow goes the dog. Do you want to play? *(Exits.)*

(SOAPHEAD CHURCH enters. He wears an oversized coat and hat. He is very old.)

SOAPHEAD CHURCH. Once there was a man who loved things. He loved things because the slightest contact with people made him sick to his stomach. All his life he had a fondness for things. *(SOAPHEAD pulls objects out of the folds of his coat as he talks. He affectionately sorts and polishes the "things.")*

CLAUDIA. A table that had been his mother's. A welcome mat from the door of the rooming house he once lived in. A quilt from a Salvation Army store counter. The residue of humanity left on the old objects replaced the physical and emotional holes of actually being touched.

SOAPHEAD CHURCH. He abhorred flesh on flesh. Body odor, breath odor, the sight of dried matter in the corner of an eye, decayed or missing teeth, ear wax, blackheads, moles, blisters, any kind of the many disgusting natural secretions the human body was capable of disgusted him to the core. His attentions therefore gradually settled on those humans whose bodies were least offensive—children.

CLAUDIA. His disdain for people led him into a profession designed to serve them. He became a:

CLAUDIA/SOAPHEAD. "Reader, Adviser, and Interpreter of Dreams."

SOAPHEAD CHURCH. It was a good life. He had a steady clientele, a decent income for a man of humble needs. He rented a small apartment from Bertha Reese, a deeply religious old lady who was clean, quiet, and very close to deafness.

CLAUDIA. There was only one problem.

SOAPHEAD CHURCH. A very big problem.

CLAUDIA. A big problem for Soaphead anyway.

SOAPHEAD CHURCH. Bertha Reese's mangy nasty old dog Bob.

CLAUDIA. The dog was as quiet and deaf as Bertha...

SOAPHEAD CHURCH. But the most nasty, revolting sight you've ever seen. He slept most of his days away on the porch in front of the door. His beady eyes ran with a sea-green matter around which gnats and flies clustered.

CLAUDIA. Soaphead prayed for the dog to hurry up and die.

SOAPHEAD CHURCH. A humane wish. He could not bear to see a creature suffer so.

CLAUDIA. It did not occur to Soaphead that his "humane" death wish for the dog was actually a reflection of his own suffering.

(SOAPHEAD produces a small paper bag.)

SOAPHEAD CHURCH. Soaphead decided to put an end to the animal's misery and bought some poison with which to do it. *(He removes the bottle of poison from the bag, opens a white parcel of meat, and puts the poison on the meat. He then pockets the meat and the poison.)*

CLAUDIA. Only the horror of having to go near the dog prevented Soaphead from completing his mission.

SOAPHEAD. And so he waited for rage or blinding revulsion to give him the courage to do what must be done.

CLAUDIA. And it was in the middle of this wait that a barely pregnant Pecola made her way to Soaphead's front door.

(Enter PECOLA. CLAUDIA exits.)

SOAPHEAD CHURCH. What can I do for you, my child?

PECOLA. It true you help people get they wishes, Mr. Church?

SOAPHEAD CHURCH. Call me Soaphead Church. Everybody else does.

PECOLA. So you can help, Mr.... *(Beat.)* You can help me.

SOAPHEAD CHURCH. Says so right here. *(Pulling a card out of his coat, handing it to her.)* Satisfaction guaranteed.

PECOLA. Maybe, maybe you can do it for me.

SOAPHEAD CHURCH. What do you need me to do?

PECOLA. I can't go to school no more. And I thought maybe you could help me.

SOAPHEAD CHURCH. Tell me. *(Pause.)*

PECOLA. My eyes. *(Beat.)* I want them blue. I want them blue so people won't turn away from me when I walk down the street. So I can go to school. So my stomach stop growing and my baby be strong. I want them blue so my mama love me and I have friends and they think I'm pretty. I want them blue so people don't do ugly things in front of me and I stop being invisible.

(Long pause. SOAPHEAD is moved. He thinks.)

SOAPHEAD CHURCH. Kneel, my child. *(PECOLA kneels. SOAPHEAD makes a sign of the cross over her.)* I work only through the Lord. If He wants your wish granted, he will do it. *(He stops, still in thought. He removes a rosary from his pocket. Looks at it. Discards it. He removes a Bible from another pocket. Rifles through it. Discards it as well. Finally he removes the white parcel of poisoned meat. Only then does the idea occur to him.)* We must make some offering, that is, some contact with nature. Perhaps some simple creature might be the vehicle through which He will speak. Let us see. *(SOAPHEAD blesses the meat as he has just blessed*

PECOLA and hands it to her.) Take this parcel and give it to the creature sleeping on the front porch. Make sure he eats it all. And mark well how he behaves. If nothing happens, you will know that God has refused you. If the animal behaves strangely, your wish will be granted on the day following this one.

PECOLA. Thank you, Mr. Soaphead. *(PECOLA takes the parcel. She nods and exits.)*

Scene v

(PECOLA stands center stage, in her own tight light.)

PECOLA. I walk past Mr. Soaphead's porch every Tuesday, Thursday and Friday when I helped Mrs. Breedlove with the laundry, so I knowed that dog. I liked that dog. People say he a ugly dog. I don't see why...his brown fur a little uneven in some places, even a little pink skin show through, and one of his ears look like it got bit off, maybe by some neighborhood bully dog...but he had soft eyes that would look at you and ask you to love him. I liked to pet him and sometime I even would give him a Mary Jane candy as a special treat. He was happy to see me. He looked up at me and his eyes were softer than I had ever seed them, and he licked the back of my hand like he was grateful just that I saw him...just that I took the time to pat him on his head. He gobbled the meat in the parcel up in one big gulp...and then it all happened quicker than I thought anything could happen. He barked and the bark turned into a cough, then into a horrible whine like a scream almost...then his eyes rolled back up into his head and he started to panting, trying to catch his breath, and scratching at the ground, all the time looking at me like it was my fault...like how could I do that to him. Like I'm his only friend in the world and how could I...and then he was just quiet and he stopped and lay there. Right there at my feet. And everything was quiet. *(Long pause.)* And I think...I guess this what Mr. Soaphead mean. And I go to try to find me a mirror.

Scene vi

(SOAPHEAD sits at a table. Folds his hands as if in prayer, then takes out paper and pen. He writes the following:)

SOAPHEAD CHURCH. Dear God:

The purpose of this letter is to familiarize you with facts which either have escaped your notice, or which you have chosen to ignore. A little black girl came to me.

Do you know what she came for? She came for blue eyes. New blue eyes, she said. Like she was buying shoes. "I'd like a pair of new blue eyes." She must have asked you for them for a very long time, and you haven't replied. She came to me. Did you forget about the children? Did you? Yes. You forgot. You let them go wanting, sit on road shoulders, crying next to their dead mothers. I've seen them charred, lame, halt. You forgot, Lord. You forgot how and when to be God.

That's why I changed the little black girl's eyes for her, and I didn't touch her. Not a finger did I lay on her. But I gave her those blue eyes she wanted. Not for pleasure and not for money. I did what You did not, could not, would not do.

I, I have caused a miracle. I gave her the eyes. Cobalt blue. A streak of it right out of your own blue heaven. No one else will see her blue eyes, but she will. And she will live happily every after. I, I have found it meet and right so to do.

With kindest regards, I remain, Your Elihue Micah Whitcomb, aka Soaphead Church.

(SOAPHEAD folds the sheets of paper, puts them into an envelope and seals it with sealing wax.

Light dims and rises on PECOLA, standing with a mirror.)

Scene vii

GIRLS IN V.O. Look. Look. Here comes a friend. The friend will play with Jane. They will play a good game. Play, Jane. Play.

(A very pregnant PECOLA has a conversation with an imaginary friend. The voice of the friend is her own voice in V.O.)

P. VOICE. How many times a minute you gone look at that old thing?

PECOLA. I didn't look a long time.

P. VOICE. You did too—

PECOLA. So what. I can look if I want to.

P. VOICE. I didn't say you couldn't. Just don't know why you have to look every minute. They aren't going anywhere.

PECOLA. I know it. I just like to look.

P. VOICE. You scared they might go away?

PECOLA. Of course not. How can they go away?

P. VOICE. The others went away.

PECOLA. Did not. They just changed.

P. VOICE. Go away. Change. What's the difference?

PECOLA. A lot. Mr. Soaphead Church said they would last forever.

P. VOICE. Forever and ever amen?

PECOLA. Yes, if you want to know.

P. VOICE. You don't have to be all smarty when you talk to me.

PECOLA. I wasn't bein' smarty.

P. VOICE. I'd just like to do something else 'sides watch you stare at that mirror all day.

PECOLA. You're just jealous.

P. VOICE. Am not.

PECOLA. You are. You wish you had them.

P. VOICE. Hah. What I look like with blue eyes?

PECOLA. Nothin' much.

P. VOICE. If you gone keep this up, I may as well go off by myself.

PECOLA. No. Don't go. Whatchu want to do?

P. VOICE. We could go outside and play, I guess.

PECOLA. Too hot.

P. VOICE. Fine! You just take your old mirror, put it in your coat pocket and you can look at yourself up and down the street.

PECOLA. You are jealous.

P. VOICE. So what, so I am jealous.

PECOLA. Are my eyes really very nice?

P. VOICE. Yes. Very nice.

PECOLA. Just "very nice"?

P. VOICE. Really, truly very nice.

PECOLA. Really, truly, bluely nice? The truly bluest eye?

P. VOICE. Oh God, you're crazy.

PECOLA. I am not! Say it!

P. VOICE. Fine! Truly bluely nice.

PECOLA. You don't have to be all mean about it.

P. VOICE. I didn't mean it mean…

PECOLA. They all try to pretend they don't see them, you know. Can you imagine? Something like that happening to a person and nobody, but nobody saying anything about it.

P. VOICE. They're probably just jealous too.

PECOLA. You are the only one who tells me how pretty they are.

P. VOICE. Yes.

PECOLA. You are a real friend.

P. VOICE. Yes. Yes. I am.

(Light fades on PECOLA. CLAUDIA steps forward.)

CLAUDIA. And so is the how and the edges of the why of it. A little black girl yearns for the blue eyes of a little white girl, and horror of the heart of her yearning is ex-

ceeded only by the evil of fulfillment. A little black girl
steps over into madness, a madness which protected her
from us, simply because in the end it bored us.

(FRIEDA enters, joins CLAUDIA.)

CLAUDIA. I talk about how I did not plant the seeds too
deeply, how it was the fault of the earth, the land, of our
town. I even think now that the land of the entire country was hostile to marigolds that year. This soil is bad
for certain kinds of flowers. Certain seeds it will not
nurture, certain fruit it will not bear, and when the land
kills of its own volition, we acquiesce and say the victim
had no right to live. We are wrong, of course, but it
doesn't matter. It's too late.

FRIEDA. At least on the edge of our town,

CLAUDIA. Among the garbage and the sunflowers of our
town, it's much, much, much too late.

(Lights fade. END PLAY.)